How the World Began

and other stories of Creation

How the World Began

and other stories of Creation

Andrew Matthews

illustrated by

Sheila Moxley

This edition first published in Great Britain in 1996 by
Macdonald Young Books
61 Western Road
Hove, East Sussex BN3 1JD

Text © Andrew Matthews 1996
Illustrations © Sheila Moxley 1996

For Mary, Ian, Pat, Dylan and Tom

Edited by Nicola Barber
Designed by Martin Lovelock
Printed in Portugal

British Library Cataloguing in Publication Data available

ISBN 07500 1606 X

Contents

Introduction

This is a book of beginnings, and a book of endings.

No-one knows who first asked where the world came from – it is a question as old as humankind – but this is a book of answers to that question. The answers come from different peoples who lived in different places at different times.

Humans have always been creators. In ancient times they took bits of stone and pieces of bone and fashioned them into tools, they moulded clay into pots and shaped lumps of amber into necklaces. People made what they wanted from things they found in the world about them, and they came to the conclusion that the world itself had been made and shaped by a creator. So they told stories to explain how and why that making and shaping happened. Sometimes the stories went on to tell what would happen when the world came to an end, but there was never really an ending, for out of the destruction a new beginning always came, and the new world was always better than the one that had gone before.

In my retellings, I have adapted the source material in order to make the stories clearer. While some of these adaptations are very free, I hope I have stayed true to the spirit of the originals.

The Seven Days

from The Old Testament of the Bible

Jehovah created the world. At first it was all one ocean, flat and dark. Jehovah moved through the darkness over the waters.

'Let light come into the world,' he said, and at the sound of his voice a brightness flashed out upon the ocean. The brightness was the first day of the world, and Jehovah used the darkness to make the first night.

On the second day, Jehovah made the sky. It shone dazzlingly blue. Clouds towered up and dropped thin veils of rain into the ocean, so that there was water on the world.

On the third day, Jehovah raised land from out of the ocean. The land was bare. The mountains looked like broken teeth biting into the sky. Jehovah breathed on the land and grass spread out in a green wave. Herbs, vines and fruit trees came out of the ground and filled the air with sweet smells.

On the fourth day, Jehovah made the Sun to move across

the blue sky of day and to warm the land with its fiery, golden light. For the night, Jehovah made the white and shadowy Moon and he sprinkled the darkness with stars.

On the fifth day, Jehovah made the creatures of the sea and air. Fish swam silver in the ocean and whales spouted rolling jets of water high into the air. Gulls and albatrosses wheeled in the sky above and, in the jungle darkness, parrots screeched as they preened their bright feathers.

On the sixth day, Jehovah made the animals of the land. They rose out of the earth like strange shoots, crawling, creeping, galloping and hopping. The air was loud with the noise of their roaring and braying. Then Jehovah said,

'I will create humans to share the beauty of the world.'

He made a beautiful garden, filled with flowers and fruit trees. Then he breathed on the ground and his breath whirled

some dust up into the shapes of Adam, the first man, and Eve, the first woman.

'This garden is called Eden,' Jehovah told them. 'Guard it well. It is filled with delicious fruits for you to eat. But do not eat the fruit of the Tree of Knowledge.'

Then on the seventh day, Jehovah rested from his great work.

All was happy in Eden until the day the Serpent came to the garden. The Serpent was jealous of the beautiful place Jehovah had made for Adam and Eve. It hid in the branches of the Tree of Knowledge and waited for the man and woman to walk by, then it slid down, coiling itself around the trunk of the tree.

'Why do you never eat the fruit of this tree?' it hissed.

'Because Jehovah has forbidden it,' replied Eve.

'Foolish woman!' said the Serpent. 'If you eat this fruit, you and Adam will both become gods like Jehovah!'

Eve believed the Serpent. She picked a fruit from the Tree of Knowledge, ate half of it and gave the other half to Adam.

As soon as they had eaten the fruit, Adam and Eve realized that they were naked, and for the first time they felt ashamed. They took leaves from a fig tree and covered their nakedness. When Jehovah saw them, he was very angry.

'You have eaten the fruit from the Tree of Knowledge,' he thundered. 'Because of your disobedience, you must now go out into the wild world.'

So Adam and Eve left the Garden of Eden for ever. They had gained knowledge of good and evil – but they had lost paradise.

A New Heaven and a New Earth

The Vision of St John

Lord Jehovah saw that the end of Time had come, and he knew that he must undo the world he had made. Jehovah gave a book closed with seven seals to the Lamb of God, the Lamb with seven horns and seven eyes.

The Lamb broke open the seals, and four riders appeared. The first rider was Conquest, and he rode a white horse.

The second rider was War and his horse was red. The third was Famine, on a horse as black as night, and the fourth rider's name was Death. His horse was sickly green and he was followed by a darkness like the shadow in the mouth of a grave. The riders galloped through the world, bringing destruction wherever they went.

The golden Sun darkened and the Moon turned as red as blood. The stars fell to the Earth like ripe figs falling from a tree. The blue sky vanished as though it had been rolled up like a scroll. Earthquakes shook the land, volcanoes erupted with spouts of fire, and thunder crashed across the heavens as the lightning danced.

All the kings and rulers of the world were terrified. They hid themselves in caves and begged the rocks and mountains to hide them from Jehovah's anger.

The Children
of Atum

from the stories told by the Ancient Egyptians

At the beginning of the beginning was Nun. Nun was an ocean. It was still and silent. It stretched out into the darkness forever and there was nowhere, because all places were the same.

And then a voice was heard in the silence.

'I am Atum,' it said.

The god Atum appeared. He had created himself by saying his name aloud. His shining Eye sent out rays of light that cut

through the darkness like a sharp sword and
made the wide waters glitter.

Atum flew over Nun looking for a place to rest because
creating himself had used up almost all of his strength.

'There must be somewhere,' he cried.

At the sound of these words a hill rose out of the water. The
hill was round and smooth, like a shoulder. Atum rested on
the hill and, when he felt strong again, he made Shu, god of
wind and breath, and Tefnut, goddess of water.

'You will make the world,' Atum told Shu and Tefnut. 'Your children will be the earth and the sky. But before you have children, go and play – for you are gods.'

Shu and Tefnut flew across the dark waters of Nun. Far away they went, laughing and playing together, but when they grew tired of playing they found that they were lost. They did not know the way back to Atum.

Atum waited impatiently for Shu and Tefnut. When they did not return, Atum sent his Eye to look for them, sweeping the darkness with its bright rays. For a long time, blind Atum waited in darkness. Slowly he grew another Eye. He saw the hill beneath him and the ocean all around. Far off, there was a glimmer of light. It was his first Eye, bringing Shu and Tefnut back to him.

As they drew closer, Atum called out to his first Eye, 'You will travel through the sky of the world to come, and be

its light. You will be
called the Sun and your
warmth will waken Ra, the
greatest of the gods!'

Atum embraced Shu and Tefnut. He
was so happy they had come back to him that
he wept tears of joy, and his tears turned into the
first people of the world.

Atum made the land rise up out of the ocean. He
covered the land with trees and flowers, and gave the
people crops to plant, and animals to herd and hunt.

'Care for this world as I care for you,' Atum said.

And the people sang their praise to the god who had
given them life.

19

The Anger of Ra

As the great god Ra grew old, he became frail. His eyes dimmed and his hair turned white. Though people still prayed to him, their prayers were not always answered. Harvests failed, and famine spread through the land of Egypt. Plagues

ravaged the cities and the streets were littered with the dead.

The high priests and rulers of Egypt met in secret.

'Ra has lost his power to protect us,' they said. 'We no longer need him. We must make a plan to overthrow him and rule the world in his place.'

But Ra heard their whisperings, and he burned with rage. He summoned his daughter Sekhmet, the lion-goddess.

Marduk the Mighty

from the stories told by the Ancient Babylonians

In the deep beginning everything was silent and nothing changed. Apsu, the god of the fresh-water ocean slept next to his wife Tiamat, goddess of the salt-water ocean. Above them floated the misty shapes of their sons, Mummu and Kingu.

And then from out of the oceans came the twin gods Lahnu and Lahanu. They laughed and played in the quiet darkness, and they had two children, Anshar and Kishar. Anshar made

24

the place where the Earth touches the sky. Kishar made the place where the sky touches the Earth. From where these two places meet came Anu, god of the sky and Ea, god of the earth and water. Anu filled the sky with howling wind and thunder. He made lightning crackle across the black clouds. Ea made huge waves that crashed on the earth, and fiery volcanoes that rumbled and smoked.

Apsu, Tiamat, Mummu and Kingu awoke.

'These new gods are noisy!' Mummu said to Apsu. 'It was peaceful before they came. If we kill them we can listen to the silence again.'

But Ea heard Apsu and Mummu talking. Ea was cunning, and he knew how to trap the fresh-water god. First he froze Apsu into ice and then he turned him into rivers and lakes and killed him. Then Ea tied Mummu up and used his body as the foundation for a secret palace, underground. Hidden in his palace, Ea took some mud and moulded it into a shape. He breathed life into the shape until it became his wife, Daminka. She gave birth to a son. His name was Marduk.

When Tiamat heard that Apsu was dead, she was very angry. From the boiling of her fury she made a great army of monsters – scorpion-men, lion-men and flying dragons. Tiamat gave the army to her son, Kingu. To make Kingu strong, she also gave him the Stones of Fate on which was written all that had been and all that was to be. Then Tiamat and Kingu set out with their army to destroy the new gods.

The battle raged for many days. The sky was dark with dragons and the air was filled with the roaring of the lion-

men. The younger gods fought hard with their war clubs, but no matter how many monsters they killed, more came to take their place. Finally, Anu, god of the sky, ran in desperation to Marduk.

'We are doomed to die unless you can save us, Marduk,' he said. 'You are the youngest and strongest of us all. Take the last of our powers and challenge Tiamat to single combat.'

So Marduk filled himself with volcano fire. He made bows and arrows from the wind and rain and a war-club from a bolt of white lightning. Marduk wove seven hurricanes into a net and rode out in a chariot of storms.

'Tiamat!' he cried. 'Come and fight me, face to face!'

Tiamat ran forward to meet Marduk. She sent a great wave to drown him, but Marduk struck the wave with his club of lightning and the water hissed into foam. Marduk rode his dark chariot round Tiamat, firing arrows into her until one finally pierced her heart and she fell down dead. The army of monsters wailed in despair and turned to flee, but Marduk threw his hurricane-net over them, and none escaped. Marduk took Kingu prisoner and siezed the Stones of Fate.

Marduk used half of Tiamat's body to create the stars, Moon and Sun. With the other half he created the world. He built homes for the younger gods in the air and earth and water.

Then Marduk killed Kingu, and from his blood he made people to help the gods look after the world. The people built temples to the gods and prayed to them. The greatest of all these temples was in the city of Babylon, and it was the temple dedicated to Marduk the Mighty.

The Great Flood

In the ancient land of Mesopotamia, the great city of Shurrupak stood on the banks of the River Euphrates. Here the gods lived in beautiful temples, and because Shurrupak was a holy city, it prospered.

But in time the city grew too large. The clamour of the people in the streets was so loud that it disturbed the gods' rest. The people became proud. Their riches made them forget to pray and give offerings to the gods.

The gods met in angry council. Angriest of all was Enlil.

'All day and night the people bellow like wild animals!' he declared. 'Sleep is impossible. Our temples are empty and humankind has lost all respect for us. I will send a famine to reduce the numbers of people so that we can have peace.'

So Enlil dried up all the rivers, and took the clouds from the sky. No rain fell. Crops withered in the fields. Soon the people of Shurrupak began to die of thirst and hunger.

But still there was no peace. The suffering people shrieked and wailed so much that the gods could find no rest.

'Enough!' cried Enlil. 'I will send a great flood to destroy humankind and wash the Earth clean of their memory.'

Now, in Shurrupak there was one man who had stayed faithful to the god Ea. His name was Utnapishtim, and every day he prayed and made offerings at Ea's temple. When Ea heard of Enlil's plan, he visited Utnapishtim's house at night and spoke to him in a voice like the whispering of the wind through a bed of reeds.

'A great flood is coming,' Ea whispered. 'Tear down your house and use the wood to build a boat. Make it big enough for you and your family and all the creatures of the Earth. Set a roof over the top and seal the wood with pitch so no water can come in – but tell no-one that it was I who gave you warning, for if Enlil hears of it, you will perish!'

Utnapishtim obeyed Ea. He built the boat and filled it with animals and all the treasures of his house.

Utnapishtim's neighbours thought he had gone mad. 'What are you doing?' they asked.

'Enlil is angry with me,' replied Utnapishtim. 'He has banished me from the city. I am going to make my home on the sea.'

In all, it took seven days to make and load the boat. On the evening of the seventh day, the Lords of Hell set the land alight with flaming torches. The cries and screams of the people were drowned out by a mighty clap of thunder – and then the rains came.

There had never been such rain before. It crashed down on the Earth in a great wave, and all the people of Shurrupak were

Izanagi and Izanami

from the Shinto legends of Japan

In the beginning there was Heaven and the ocean. The ocean was so salty that its water was as white as clouds. Patches of weed floated on the milky-white water, but there were neither waves nor wind. All was still and quiet.

The High Lord of Heaven made Izanagi and Izanami to be man and wife. When Izanagi and Izanami stood before him, he held out a spear to them. The spear was set with jewels that glowed like flames.

'The world is still and nothing changes,' said the High Lord. 'Take this spear and make the land, so there can be life and death, sorrow and joy.'

Izanagi and Izanami took the spear and went to stand on the Bridge of Heaven. They dipped the tip of the spear into the ocean and stirred. The jewels flashed coloured light over the white water. Light and water and weeds swirled and danced faster and faster.

Then Izanagi and Izanami lifted the spear. Seven drops of water fell from it and formed the seven floating islands of Japan.

Izanagi and Izanami made children to fill the world. Their children were the Sun and Moon, mountains, storm and fire. Waves rose up from the ocean and crashed on to the shores of the seven islands, grinding the rocks into shining sand. Lightning flickered on the tops of the mountains and rain fell. Plants sprang from the earth. Grass and flowers grew. Pine forests whispered in the wind, and cherry trees blossomed white and pink.

Izanagi and Izanami stepped down from the Bridge of Heaven and walked in the world they had made. Its beauty filled their hearts with joy, and they laughed like thunder.

Luonnatar the Lonely

from the Finnish epic, The Kalevala

In the beginning there was the sky, and beneath it an ocean without end. Through the desert of the sky, Luonnatar drifted. She was filled with loneliness and longing. For seven hundred years she travelled the sky, seeing nothing and no-one.

In despair, Luonnatar drifted down on to the ocean and floated on the waves. The ocean currents carried her here and there, but wherever Luonnatar went there was nothing to see. Her loneliness grew until it gnawed like sharp teeth.

'Is there nothing else?' she cried out.

Her voice carried over the ocean. The words grew white feathers and wings. The sound of Luonnatar's voice became a white bird. It circled round her and landed on one of her knees.

The white bird built a nest from its down and laid two eggs. The eggs were hot. They burned Luonnatar's skin. She tried to lie still, but the pain was too much and she dipped her knee under the water to cool it.

The eggs were washed away. They sank down into the dark depths of the ocean, then broke open in a blaze of light. The bottom halves of the shells formed the Earth and the top halves became the heavens. The golden yolks turned into the Sun and the whites turned into the Moon and stars and clouds.

Luonnatar swam ashore and began shaping the world. She heaped rocks into mountains to hold up the sky. She shaped coastlines and hollowed out the sea bed. All the time, the white bird fluttered round her, singing sweetly.

So Luonnatar made the world from her loneliness and emptiness, while the white bird sang a song of making, and the new Sun and Moon shone down upon her.

The Coming of the Gods

from the myths of the Ancient Greeks

Before the world, there was Chaos. In Chaos, everything that might be and could never be whirled in a storm. Dark chased after light, fire and water spun together, and everywhere there was movement and change. The only stillness was at the centre of the storm, where there was nothing.

Out of Chaos and into that nothing burst Gea, the Earth. The storm tried to pull her back, but Gea clung tightly to the still centre and remained. Gea made Uranos, the sky, and crowned him with the Sun, Moon and stars. Uranos took Gea

36

as his mate. Showers of his rain fell down on Gea and made grass grow over her hills and plains. Flowers and trees sprang from the grass. Animals roamed the land, fishes teemed in the seas and birds washed their new feathers in the rain.

Gea's first children were three giants, each with a hundred hands. As soon as they were born they set to work, piling up the mountains and carving out the rocky valleys of Greece.

Gea's next three children were also giants – the one-eyed Cyclopses. They worked underground, forging metal in the fiery furnaces of volcanoes. They made the Underworld, and the deep pit of Tartarus.

Then Gea bore six more male and six more female children. These were the Titans. They were proud and strong, but one was prouder and stronger than the rest. His name was Cronos.

When Uranos saw how powerful his children were, he grew afraid. He threw the Titans into the black pit of Tartarus, and waited for them to die.

Cronos lay in the darkness, feeling his hatred for Uranos grow stronger. He called out to Gea, and the other Titans took up his cry. Gea heard the voices of her children and a great pain filled her. When it was night and Uranos was asleep, she went down to the Underworld and freed the Titans. To Cronos, she gave a sharp sickle made from one of her own flint bones.

'Use this sickle to take revenge upon your father,' she whispered. 'Go quickly, while he is still asleep!'

Cronos left the Underworld and ran swiftly to the mountain where Uranos lay. Moving more quietly than a shadow, Cronos crept up on the sleeping Uranos. He raised the flint sickle so that its blade shone white in the glow of the Moon, and then he struck his father over and over again. With his last, dying breath, Uranos spoke in a terrible voice that crackled and boomed like thunder.

'My curse on you, Cronos! You too will know how it feels to be struck down by your own child!'

Cronos laughed at these words. With his father dead, he knew that no-one was strong enough to keep him from doing whatever he wished. He threw the hundred-handed giants and the Cyclopses into Tartarus. Then he conquered the other Titans and imprisoned them in the Underworld also – except for his sister Rhea, whom he married.

Rhea bore Cronos many children, but Cronos remembered his father's curse and as each child was born he wrenched it from Rhea's arms and swallowed it. When Rhea gave birth to her last child, Zeus, she hid him in her bed. To fool Cronos, she wrapped a large stone in swaddling clothes and gave that to her husband to swallow. Then she took the infant Zeus to the island of Crete, where she hid him in a deep cave. Every night she visited him while Cronos was asleep.

Zeus grew quickly. Within three days he was as tall and strong as Cronos. Rhea told Zeus the story of his cruel father and his lost brothers and sisters. Zeus smiled.

'I can get them back', he said, 'for I am a god.'

Zeus gathered some herbs from outside his cave and brewed up a special potion.

'Pour this into my father's mouth when he falls asleep,' he told Rhea.

That night, as Cronos slept, Rhea dripped the potion into his open mouth. As soon as Cronos swallowed the potion, he disgorged the stone that had taken Zeus's place, and then the rest of Rhea's children – Hestia, Demeter, Hera, Hades and Poseidon.

Cronos fled to the Underworld. He freed the Titans and begged them to help him fight the gods. A bitter war followed. The Titans tore down mountains and threw them at their enemies. Cronos struggled with his children, slashing at them with his flint sickle. The gods were strong, but not even they had the power to overcome Cronos and the Titans. And then, while both sides were resting from the battle, Zeus had a

cunning idea. He went down into the depths of Tartarus and freed the Cyclopses. To show their gratitude they made him a deadly weapon, the thunderbolt. Zeus grasped the thunderbolt firmly and its white fire crackled around his fingers. From far above came the faint sounds of fighting.

Zeus returned to the battle. The first thunderbolt that Zeus threw struck Cronos on the head and killed him instantly. The other Titans immediately gave up the fight. They knew that they could not stand against Zeus and his thunderbolts.

Some of the Titans were sent to an island in the Western Ocean where they were guarded by the hundred-handed giants; others were thrown back into Tartarus. However, a different fate awaited one of the Titans, called Atlas. He was condemned to carry the weight of the sky on his back forever.

When all this was done, Zeus and the other gods and goddesses stood on the summit of Mount Olympus and gazed out at the beautiful world they had won.

Walking Man

from the legends of the Pima tribe in Arizona

In the beginning there was only darkness, dust and water. The darkness was thicker in some places than in others. In one place it was so thick that it made a man. The man walked through the darkness. After a while, he began to think.

'I'm walking, but where am I going?' thought Walking Man. 'I must make somewhere.'

Walking Man took a handful of dust and mixed it with some water. He made the dust and the water into a ball which he rolled along with his foot.

'It's time to make the world
For me to walk in, as I must,' he sang.
'It's time for me to make the world
From water and from dust.'

He sang slowly. While he sang, the rolling ball got bigger and bigger. When Walking Man stopped singing, the world was finished.

'Ha!' said Walking Man. 'There's too much darkness for me to see the world.'

He dipped his hands into a pool and shook drops of water from his fingers. They stuck on the darkness and made the stars. The stars sparkled, but there was not enough light for Walking Man to see the world.

So he took water and dust, and mixed them together to make clay. Then he moulded the clay into a bowl. He put water and starlight into the bowl and stirred them together. When they were spinning, he threw them up into the stars and made the Moon. The Moon glowed palely, but there was still not enough light for Walking Man to see the world.

So he made two bowls. He filled one bowl with water and the glow of the Moon, then put the other bowl on top so the glow couldn't get away. Then he breathed on the bowls and waited for a long time.

The Moon's glow and the water and Walking Man's breath turned into the Sun. The bowls cracked and rays of light streamed out into the darkness.

Walking Man took the Sun and threw it high. The dark turned into the sky and everything was bright. At last Walking Man could see the world. He saw green forests and blue oceans and mountains with white tops, and they made him smile.

'This is a good world!' cried Walking Man. 'I'm glad I made it!'

And he walked off to find where he was going.

Coyote

*from the folk tales of the native North Americans of
the western and south-western United States*

At the start of things, it was dark. Dark lay on dark and all was
black and still. Then, into the stillness came a small sound, a
quiet sound. It got bigger, louder and stronger until it filled the
darkness. The sound was Coyote's howl.

Coyote grew around the howl. First came his mouth with its
sharp, white teeth, then his head with its bright eyes, then his
body, bones and fur. Last of all came a tail. Coyote blinked his
eyes at the darkness.

'My legs want to run, but I can't run through the dark!' he said.

He breathed a wind in the shape of a shell. He turned the shell upside-down and with a shake of his head he flung it into the air and made the sky.

Coyote took colours to the five corners of the Earth and then he waited. The colours grew into the sky and bent together in the first rainbow. The rainbow divided the day from the night.

Coyote howled a disc of burning gold and put it into the sky to be the Sun. He howled a disc of gleaming silver and put it into the sky to be the Moon.

'My legs want to run, but there's nothing to run on!' he said.

Coyote bared his teeth and growled. The hard sound of the growl turned into rocks and hills and mountains. Coyote growled more softly. His growl made forests and grassy prairies.

Coyote blinked his eyes at the world.

'My legs want to run, but I have no-one to run with!' he said.

So he yelped. Hares darted across the prairies, deer and bison galloped. Mice scuttled across the forest floor and great bears lumbered through the undergrowth. Coyote yelped again and salmon leapt from the rivers, beavers bustled through the water. Mountain lions padded over the hills while eagles soared above them on dark wings.

'My legs want to run, but I have no-one to run from!' said Coyote.

He found a river with a high bank made from soft, red clay.

With his sharp claws, Coyote dug in the bank and made heaps of clay. Then he breathed on them. The heaps of clay began to stir. They grew and changed shape until, finally, they became the first people.

'Wake up!' Coyote said. 'You must gather corn and fruits for food; you must hunt animals for meat. You must build tepees and fill the world with your children. And wherever you go, I shall run from you. You will never catch me, but you will hear me at night when I howl at the Moon.'

And Coyote ran through the world he had made, barking and howling for joy.

Amei Awi and Burung Une

from the Dyaks of Borneo

First there was darkness, stretching from forever to forever. In that darkness floated a little spider. She gathered some darkness in her long, thin legs and began to spin. She made a silver thread, and fastened it to the two sides of forever. Then she dangled from the thread and wove a web that glimmered in the darkness.

A flat piece of red coral, no bigger than a speck of dust, fell into the web and stuck there. Year after year the coral grew, until it was as big as the world.

Then a snail fell out out of the dark. The snail landed on the coral and crawled all over its crinkled surface. Wherever the snail crawled it left a slimy trail. The slime dried up, and as it dried it turned brown and made the soil.

Into the soil fell a sapling. The sapling pushed down its roots and stretched out its branches and grew into a tall tree. Seeds fell from the tree. They landed on the soil and sprouted. Soon the world was covered with forests.

Into one forest fell a giant crab. The crab lumbered over the flat world, squeezing the soil with its strong claws. It made hills and mountains, and deep valleys. Rain began to fall, and the valleys filled with wide rivers. The water of the rivers mixed with soil to form swamps, and in the swamps grew many plants that were good to eat.

Two beings came out of the darkness, a male and female. They had bodies, but their bodies kept shifting their shape, like smoke in the wind. The two beings took a fallen branch from the forest and carved it into two heads, then they breathed on the heads to give them life. The heads opened their eyes and began to speak. As soon as this happened, the shapeless male and female went back to the darkness from which they had first come.

The heads had children. These children had necks, and their children had bodies – but no arms and legs. They crawled over the ground like snakes. Then they had children – Amei Awi and Burung Une, the god and goddess of farming.

Amei Awi and Burung Une learned how to grow rice and fruit trees. They built a great house in the forest and turned the land around the house into the first farm.

Amei Awi and Burung Une had eight children. Their first child was the Sun, and he sailed across the sky in a canoe. Their

second child was the Moon, and she too sailed in the sky, chasing after her brother. The other six children were human beings.

For a long time the humans did nothing but sit in the sun and eat the food that their parents grew for them. At last, Amei Awi grew angry with his lazy children. He took them to a mountain that was so high, its peak touched the clouds.

'You must climb this mountain!' said Amei Awi, 'and the way you climb it will decide the fate of your children.'

Two of the humans stayed at the foot of the mountain, looking up.

'Climbing is too much hard work,' they said. 'We will sit here and do nothing.' And their children became the first kings and rulers of the world.

The other four humans set off up the mountain. Halfway to the top, two of them sat down on a rock to rest.

'We will stay here,' they said. 'We are too tired to climb any higher.' And their children became the rich landowners of the world.

The last two humans struggled through ice and snow, right to the top of the mountain. There they fell down, exhausted. Their children became the poor people of the world, who have to spend their lives toiling in the fields.

Meanwhile, Amei Awi and Burung Une worked on. The chips of tree bark that lay scattered about their house turned into chicken, goats and cattle. Some of the bark became pigs that ran squealing into the forest.

After many long years had passed, Amei Awi and Burung Une saw how people had spread all over the world, and they knew that their work was finished. They went to live deep underground in the heart of the world, and they live there still. They whisper to the roots of the crops, telling them to grow strong so that when harvest comes, the people of the world will have enough to eat.

Olodumare

from the Yoruba people of Nigeria

Olodumare was there from the start. He lived with his family in the Void where there was nothing but darkness and water. Olodumare wondered for a long time about how to make a world. At last, he thought of a way.

Olodumare breathed a giant snail-shell out of the dark and filled it with soil. He left room in the shell for his daughter, Oduduwa, but first he changed her into a pigeon. Then he changed his other daughter, Aje, into a hen. Olodumare called to his son, Obtala.

'Take this shell to the marsh at the edge of the waters and empty it out,' he said.

Obtala flew through the darkness and emptied out the shell on to the marshes. The soil came out first, heaping up into a high mountain; then came the pigeon and the hen. The birds landed on top of the mountain and started to scratch, kicking

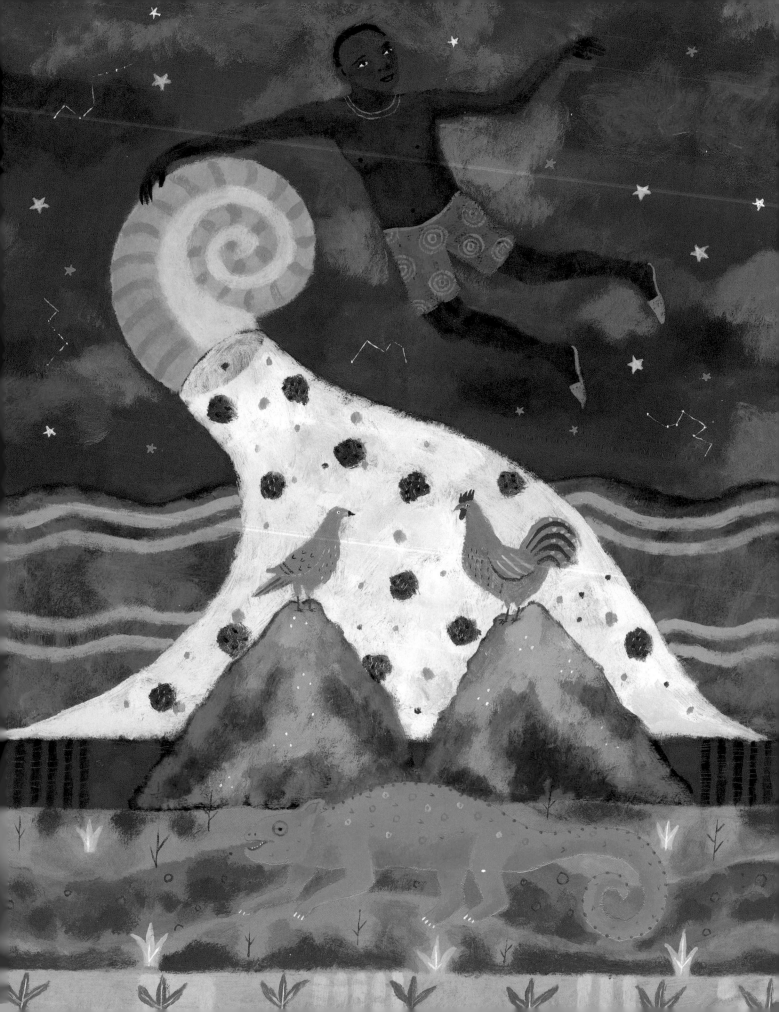

the soil behind them and scattering it to form dry land.

Olodumare made Chameleon and sent him to see if the earth was firm. Very slowly, Chameleon pressed the earth with his claw – it was still muddy. The pigeon and the hen scattered more soil and Chameleon walked on it carefully.

When Olodumare saw that Chameleon could walk without sinking into the mud he knew the ground was firm – so he made the trees. The first-ever tree was the coconut palm. Obtala made some palm wine and got so drunk that he fell down in a deep sleep. Olodumare paused to laugh at his son, then he made the oil palm and the kola nut tree.

When all the trees were made, Olodumare turned Oduduwa and Aje back into their true shapes and gave them bags of seeds.

'Scatter these all over the earth,' he told his daughters. 'I am

going to make humans and they will need crops for food.'

Then Olodumare took big handfuls of clay and shaped them into figures – eight males and eight females. He breathed on the clay and it turned into flesh, bone and blood. The figures came to life, and they were the first ancestors of the Yoruba people.

Obtala woke from his drunken sleep and went to look at the people his father had created.

'They can see nothing, they must have light,' he said to himself.

Obtala took a fallen tree from the forest and turned it into gold. He beat the golden tree with a flat disc of flint and made a jar and a boat. During the day, the golden boat floated from the top of the sky in the east to the other side in the west, carrying the glowing jar. Then Obtala turned the flint disc into the Moon so that the Yoruba people would have light during the night, too.

Great One

from the Zulu people of Natal in South Africa

In the beginning, there was darkness. Great One lay under the earth, dreaming a long, deep dream about the world. When Great One woke, he knew how things would be. He came up out of the earth carrying the Sun under one arm and the Moon under the other. He put the Sun and Moon into the sky and showed them which way to go. That was how Great One made day and night.

Great One looked at the world in the light of the Sun and he saw that it needed humans, so he took clay from the bank of a river and moulded it. The first people he made were the Bantu. He put them in the centre of the land and gave them all the things they needed to live – cattle, goats and dogs. Then Great One made white people and put them at the edge of the land, near the sea. At the same time, Great One made wild animals.

When he had done all this, Great One was weary. He wanted to send an important message to the humans, but he was too tired to take it himself. So he called Chameleon and Lizard to his side.

'Go and tell the humans that when they die it is not forever. They will come back, just like the Moon does,' he said. 'Mind you remember exactly what I have said, because a message from Great One cannot be taken back once it is spoken.'

Chameleon and Lizard set out on their journey. Chameleon moved slowly, rolling his eyes around and looking at everything. If he saw a juicy grasshopper, he opened his mouth and – zip! – out flew his long, sticky tongue to catch it. Then Chameleon would sit and eat.

Lizard moved quickly. His claws skittered over the dry stones of the road and his tail made wavy lines in the dust as he ran along. Lizard was the first to reach the humans.

'Listen to me!' said Lizard, feeling very important. 'I bring you a message from Great One.'

'What is it?' the humans asked.

Now, Lizard's thoughts scurried through his head as fast as his feet scurried over the ground. Great One's words had mixed themselves up in his mind.

'Er ... Great One wants you to know that you will all die forever!' he said.

When the humans heard this, they began to grow old. They sickened and died, crumbling back into the clay from which they were made. By the time Chameleon arrived with the real message, it was too late – Lizard's jumbled mind had brought death into the world.

Pan Ku

from the Chinese Taoist tradition

First there was darkness, nothingness. In that nothingness floated an egg, and in the egg was Pan Ku. He made himself inside the egg at the same time as he made the egg all around him.

Pan Ku floated in the egg for eighteen thousand years, and every day he grew bigger. He grew so huge that his knees and elbows pressed against the shell of the egg until it broke in two in a great burst of blinding light.

The top part of the egg was light. It floated up and made the sky. The bottom half was heavy and sank down to form the Earth. Then the sky began to fall. The sky would have crushed the Earth if Pan Ku had not stood between them. He held up

the sky with his shoulders and pressed his feet into the Earth. For thousands of years, Pan Ku stood with the weight of the sky on his shoulders, until at last the Earth and the sky were set in their places.

Holding up the sky took all Pan Ku's strength. He grew old – his skin wrinkled and his hair went white. Pan Ku was dying, but his death was the birth of the world.

Pan Ku's right eye began to burn. It flared up and became the Sun that fills the sky with brightness. His left eye glowed with a silver light and became the Moon that sails the dark sea of the night. The white hairs of his beard flew into the sky and changed into the glimmering stars.

Pan Ku's skull turned into mountains that pressed their peaks against the sky. His teeth became boulders and rocks. His flesh and bones became the soil and the rich minerals hidden in it. His hair fell on to the soil and made forests and fields, and his veins were the paths and roads that ran through them.

From Pan Ku's breath sprang the winds, and they blew around the four corners of the world that came from Pan Ku's arms and legs. His sweat dripped as rain and his voice was the loud rumble of thunder. Where the rain fell, it formed rivers and streams that flowed into the sea.

Even the fleas that had once lived on Pan Ku's body were changed – they turned into the people and animals that filled the world with their children.

So Pan Ku gave his strength and his life to make the Earth and everything in it.

Taaroa

from a Polynesian chant

In the beginning there was only Taaroa, filling all the Universe. Taaroa became lonely. The loneliness was small at first, but it grew until Taaroa could think of nothing else. He called out, but no answer came – just the echo of his own voice.

Taaroa took the echo and made a song. He sang a quiet song, a whispering song. He sang the wind blowing over the sea. The notes of the song became fish that darted in the deeps.

Taaroa changed his song to make the land. He sang white, sandy shores for the waves of the sea to break against, and rocks in the sand, and mountains above the rocks.

Taaroa's song grew louder. He sang the sky, he sang the sun and moon and stars. The sand pressed itself together to make islands of earth, and Taaroa's song fell on to the islands as seeds. Clouds gathered in the sky over the mountains and rain fell out of them. The rain watered the seeds so that they sprouted and grew into plants – trees, grass and flowers.

Taaroa sang insects, birds and animals. He sang the wings of the butterfly, the black eye of the mouse and the white feathers of the albatross. The air was filled with the sounds of their voices.

Then, when Taaroa saw that the world was ready, he sang people. He sang them from inside himself and he sang himself inside them, so they were filled with light and the music of the song of the world.

From the One

*taken from the Bridhadaranyaka Upanishad,
written in India in the 9th century B.C.*

At first, there was no today or yesterday. There was no time or place. There was only the One, thinking the deep thoughts of forever.

Then the thoughts of the One became words.

'I exist,' the One said. 'There is nothing else.'

As soon as the words were spoken the One knew it was alone, and with its loneliness came a fear and an unhappiness it could not bear.

The One split itself in two. There was darkness and light, sea and sky, mountain and valley – and the first man and

woman. The man and woman stared at one another in wonder. Instead of the loneliness the One had felt, they felt the togetherness of love. They became husband and wife, and from them came children – all the people of the world.

When the wife saw her children, she thought, 'This cannot be right. How can we two, who were once the One, have become so many?'

The wife tried to hide by turning herself into a cow, but her husband found her. He turned himself into a bull, and from the cow and the bull were born all the cattle of the world. Then the wife turned herself into a mare, but her husband became a stallion. When she took the form of a ewe, he became a ram. The wife became a tigress, a she-owl, and an ant – but every time her husband found her.

So all the animals in the world were made. Everything came from the One, and the One became everything.

The Feathered Gods

from the Popol Vuh, the sacred book of the Mayans

Before the world, there was nothing but ocean and sky. The ocean was still and the sky was dark with night. Into the darkness came the gods Tepeu and Gucamatz. They had green and blue feathers like birds, and scales like snakes. They were the wisest of the gods and they shared their wisdom. They planned the whole world, from the highest mountain to the deepest lake.

When their plans were finished, Tepeu and Gucamatz sent Hurakan, god of winds, to fly out over the black ocean.

Hurakan looked down and called out,

'Earth!'

The waters of the ocean boiled and mountains rose out of them like billows of storm cloud. In the valleys between the mountains, forests grew.

'Dawn!' cried Hurakan.

The Sun rose. Light touched the tops of the mountains. Streams flowed down the mountainsides and made rivers that wound like serpents across the plains. Fields of corn sprouted and swayed in the wind like the waves of the ocean. The ripe heads of corn gleamed golden in the

first light. In the forests, monkeys chattered and jaguars snarled. Fish swam in the rivers and the seas. Ants scurried over the earth and spiders wove their silver webs.

When they saw the beauty of the world Tepeu and Gucamatz were so happy that they danced in the sky.

'Now we must make people to live in the world!' said Gucamatz, excitedly.

Gucamatz and Tepeu went into a forest and cut thick branches from the trees. They carved the branches into the shapes of men and women and stood them on the ground.

'Hurakan!' said Tepeu, 'give these carvings life!'

Hurakan gathered the winds from all over the world. The winds blew into the mouths of the wooden figures and gave them breath. Rain fell on them and turned the wood into flesh and blood. The first people woke and looked around, but something was wrong. Their eyes were so sharp that they could

see everything. They believed that they themselves had made the world and everything in it, and they were proud.

'We need no gods,' they said. 'We will worship ourselves.'

Gucamatz and Tepeu were filled with anger. They called on Hurakan to send a great flood to wash the first people away. When the flood waters ran back into the rivers and the sea, Gucamatz and Tepeu went to the plains and gathered maize. They pounded the white and yellow grains and mixed up a paste. From the paste, they moulded the second people.

'Give them life, Hurakan!' cried Gucamatz. 'But dim their eyes so that they cannot see too far, then they will not be proud.'

So Hurakan breathed life into the people. They opened their dim eyes and saw the Feathered Gods in the sky above them.

'You are so great and we are so small,' the people said. 'We will pray to you for strength and guidance.'

And, at last, the gods were content.

The Bagadjimbiri Brothers

from the Aborigine people of Australia

In the beginning, a Dream dreamed the world. In the beginning was the Dreamtime. There was no Sun or Moon; everything was in darkness. Under the earth, the Ancestors were sleeping and their dreams were silent.

Then the Ancestors began to wake. They stretched their arms and legs and broke through the earth. At first, the Ancestors looked like men and women, but inside they had the spirits of animals and plants, rocks and winds and stars. Their spirits made them restless and they set off across the world to discover who they really were.

When the Bagadjimbiri brothers woke up from the earth, they laughed and played. They chased one another, jumping, rolling and tumbling in the dust until, finally, they turned into dingoes.

'This place is no good, brother,' one said to the other, 'it needs trees and animals.'

So the Bagadjimbiri brothers went to work. They dug in the earth with their strong claws and made the first water-holes so that life could spring up around them.

While they worked, the Bagadjimbiri brothers grew until their heads touched the sky.

'This place is too small, brother,' one said to the other. 'It's time for us to go exploring.'

They walked for many days, until they met a man called Ngariman. When he saw two giant dingoes coming towards him, Ngariman was so frightened that he hissed and yowled

and turned into a cat. Fur sprang out of his skin, and his teeth grew sharp points. His fingernails turned into claws and long whiskers sprouted under his nose.

The Bagadjimbiri brothers thought the cat was the funniest-looking creature they had ever seen. They laughed so much that they fell down, helplessly rocking with mirth.

Ngariman hated the brothers for laughing at him. He killed them and buried their bodies deep in the ground. But in the place where he buried them, a spring bubbled up. The water ran over the bodies of the Bagadjimbiri brothers and brought them back to life.

The brothers walked on until they grew old and it was time for them to die. They collapsed on the ground and their dead bodies became water snakes. But their spirits soared up into the air, forming clouds, and the clouds travelled through the sky, bringing rain and life to the dry, dead land.

Mawu and the Rainbow Snake

adapted from myths of the Dahomey and Togo peoples

At the beginning, there were no people, plants or animals. The wind did not sigh in the branches of trees, and there were no waves to crash against the shore. There was no Sun or Moon, no day or night. There was only Mawu, the Creator Spirit, and Mawu lay in a deep sleep. He floated through emptiness, dreaming about all the things that were to be. When the dream was finished, Mawu woke up and time began.

Mawu took emptiness and rolled it between his palms. He rolled it out long and thin, like a potter with a piece of clay and then he drew scales on it with his thumbnail. Mawu breathed colour on to the scales and life into them and the emptiness turned into Rainbow Snake.

Rainbow Snake opened his golden eyes and flicked out his black, forked tongue.

'What shall I do, Mawu?' he asked.

'Help me to make the world,' Mawu replied.

Mawu and Rainbow Snake made the sea, then they made the land to float on it. The land was completely flat, like a plate, and the waters of the sea did not move. The world was still and silent.

Then Mawu and Rainbow Serpent travelled through the world. Mawu piled up huge mountains, filling them with gold

and precious stones. Rainbow Snake's body dug deep trenches in the soil, and the waters of the sea ran through the trenches to form rivers and streams.

Mawu covered the Earth with thick forests and filled the forests with large animals, but so deep was his love of creating that he made too many. The trees and animals were so heavy that the land began to sink into the sea.

'Rainbow Snake!' Mawu cried. 'Hold up the land!'

Rainbow Snake twisted himself round the Earth in three thousand coils, holding it up out of the water, and there he stays to this day. At night, his scales are black, but they turn white when dawn comes, and at sunset they glow a deep orange-red.

Rainbow Snake's coils move through the strong currents of rivers and oceans. They circle the Earth, moving the stars and planets across the night sky. If the sun shines through the rain, one of his coils shines as the rainbow, and the lightning is the flashing of his scales.

Most of the time, Rainbow Snake keeps very still, but if he twitches the land trembles in an earthquake, and if he were ever to relax his coils the world would fall apart and sink under the sea.

Amma and the Nummo

from the Dogon people of Mali

Before the world began, Amma the Maker lived in Heaven. Amma built a smithy and filled its forge with fire, so that Heaven glowed red. Then he took some clay and rolled it into a ball between his hands. He placed the ball of clay into the fire of the forge.

When the ball was white hot, Amma took it from the fire and put eight rings of red copper round it, and so the Sun was made. Amma put the Sun into the sky and then he made the Moon from clay, placing eight rings of white copper round it. He put the Moon into the sky, so that it followed the Sun.

From the scraps of hot clay that were left over, Amma

made the stars. He picked them up in handfuls and flung them far out into the darkness of space where they shone like bright dust.

Amma took more clay and made the Earth. He pressed the clay out flat into the shape of a female body, with her head facing north. When Earth was made, Amma realized how lonely he was, so he breathed life into the clay woman and took her for his wife.

The first time they lay together, Earth was frightened of her new husband. Because of her fear, their first child was Jackal and he was full of wickedness. Instead of living in Heaven, Jackal hid himself on Earth, waiting for the chance to make mischief.

Next time Amma lay with Earth, she gave birth to twins, one male and one female. These were the Nummo. The tops of their bodies were shaped like humans, but their lower halves were like snakes. The Nummo's eyes burned red like the fire of Amma's forge, and their bodies were covered with glittering green hair.

'My children,' Amma told the Nummo, 'I want you to make the ancestors of all the people who will live on Earth one day. Make plants for them to grow and make animals to share the world with them, but do not show them fire. If humans have fire, they will learn the secrets of Making and challenge my power.'

The Nummo took sticks, and on the ground of Heaven they drew the outlines of two bodies, one male and one female. Then they breathed on the outlines, and the outlines became

the first man and the first woman. The man and woman lived in Heaven and the woman bore eight sets of twins, eight males and eight females.

Serau, the first man, went to the Nummo and said, 'Let me and my family go down on to the Earth so that we can plant seeds and grow food. Give us fire so that we can make things.'

'Not yet,' said the Nummo. 'Earth is not ready for you. Wait a while longer until we have found Jackal and brought him back to Heaven so he can do you no harm.'

But Serau did not want to wait. In secret, he made a granary from clay. Into the granary he put his wife and children, and all the plants and animals they would need on Earth. Then Serau crept into Amma's smithy and stole fire from the forge. He put the fire into a pair of leather bellows and hid the bellows in the granary. Serau lifted the granary, rested it on his shoulders and ran towards the rainbow that joins Heaven to Earth.

The Nummo saw Serau running away and they were angry. 'Come back!' they shouted. 'Earth is not ready!'

But Serau would not listen. He jumped on to the rainbow and began to slide down it towards Earth.

The Nummo threw thunder and lightning at him. The roaring thunder dazed Serau, and when a bolt of lightning struck him, he tumbled off the rainbow. The granary fell from his shoulders, scattering people, animals and seeds everywhere.

When Serau crashed on to the Earth, he broke his arms and legs, and ever since humankind's arms and legs have bent at the knees and elbows.

Humans were spread over every part of Earth, but wherever they were Jackal sniffed them out and made trouble. He taught people different languages, so they could not understand one another. He told them lies that filled their minds with fear and hate. He made weapons and showed people how to kill, and to make war. That is why the people of the world cannot live together in peace, because Serau would not wait until the Earth was ready.

How Darkness Came

from the Kono people of Sierra Leone

God made the sky and the Earth and the sea. He filled the sky with birds, he filled the Earth with plants and animals, and he filled the sea with fish. When the world was new-made, the Sun and Moon burned so brightly in the sky that there was no cold and no dark. The plants and animals did not have shadows, and there was no night.

Then God created darkness. It was black and it made God's fingers cold when he touched it. God did not know what he had made and he could see no use for it, so he put the darkness into a small basket, covered the basket with a lid and called Bat to him.

'Bat,' God said, 'I want you to take this basket of darkness up to the Moon. Tell her to keep it somewhere safe until I decide what to do with it.'

Bat wanted to please God, so he flew off with the basket in his claws. At first, he flew quickly, but he had never flown to the Moon before. It was much further away than he thought. The basket seemed to get heavier and heavier and before long Bat was very tired and hungry.

'I must rest and have some food,' Bat said to himself. He flew down on to the ground, placed the basket at the side of the road and went into the forest to find something to eat.

While Bat was in the jungle, Leopard and Hyena came walking along the road. They saw the basket and stopped to sniff it.

'I wonder what's inside?' said Leopard.

'Food!' said Hyena, licking his lips. 'And it must be fine food to be in such a fine basket! Let's open it up and take a look!'

Leopard put out his long claws, scratched the lid off the basket and peered inside.

'What kind of food is it?' asked Hyena.

'I don't know,' said Leopard. 'I can't see anything.'

Hyena came to look, but he could not see anything either. 'Let's see if we can feel anything,' he said.

Both animals reached inside the basket, and the cold darkness stuck to them. When they pulled out their paws, Hyena and Leopard looked at the ground in horror.

'What are these black things stuck to our feet?' barked Hyena, staring at their shadows.

'Let's run away from them!' roared Leopard.

As he turned to flee into the forest, Leopard's tail lashed the basket and tipped it over. Darkness spilled out of it. The darkness spread into the forest, making it cool and gloomy. It ran into caves and filled them up with blackness. It stuck to all the plants and animals as shadows, and then it rose up into the sky to make night.

When Bat came back and saw what had happened, he was afraid that God would be angry with him.

'I must try to put all the darkness back into the basket so I can carry it to the Moon!' he said.

Now Bat sleeps through the day. When evening comes, Bat wakes up and flies through the sky, fluttering this way and that as he tries to capture all the darkness and return it to the basket – but he never succeeds. Each morning, day interrupts him before his work is finished.

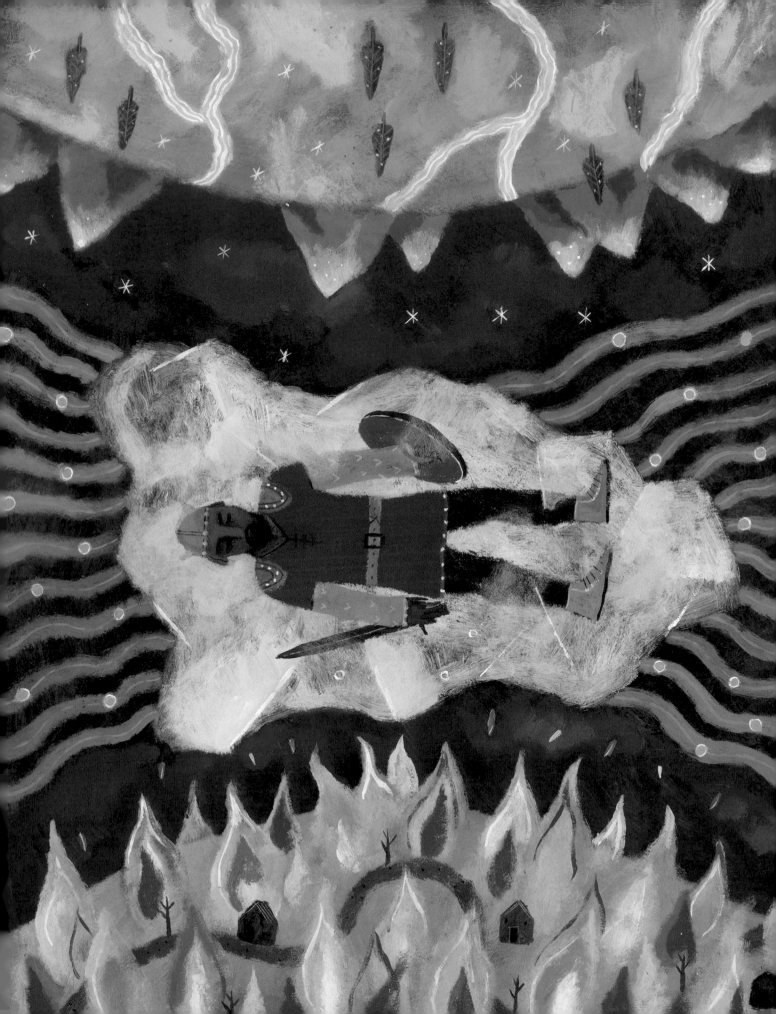

Fire and Ice

from the Norse Myths

In the beginning there was north and south, and in-between.

South was Muspellheim, the land of fire. In that land flames flicked and roared while fountains of sparks danced up into a red, glowing sky. North was Niflheim, the land of cold, where all was ice and snow. Mountains of ice stood like wolves' fangs against the black sky. Across fields of snow ran ice rivers, creaking, grinding and grumbling as they flowed through the white darkness.

In-between was Ginnungagap, the land of thaw. Sparks from Muspellheim met ice from Niflheim and the heat thawed the ice to form a sea. In that sea floated the giant Ymir, frozen and helpless inside a huge iceberg.

On the shores of the sea lived Audumla, the first cow. She liked the taste of the salty sea-ice. She licked around Ymir's feet, and up sprang the cruel Frost Giants with their white eyes and spiky hair.

Audumla licked around Ymir's arms. Her warm tongue melted the ice into strange shapes that became the gods Odin, Vili and Ve.

The gods killed Ymir and used his body to make Middle Earth, which people call the world. From Ymir's blood, the gods made seas, lakes and rivers. Soil came from Ymir's flesh and his bones were fashioned into mountains. His teeth formed boulders and rocks.

The gods took Ymir's eyebrows for a wall to keep out the greedy Frost Giants who wanted the new world for their own. Ymir's skull formed the dark bowl of the sky. The gods commanded Day and Night to chase one another across the sky in chariots, accompanied by their children, Sun and Moon.

When all this was done, the gods went walking beside the Northern Sea. Near the shore they came across two trees. They made these trees into the man, Askr, and the woman, Embla. The gods gave the man and woman sight and hearing, taste, touch and smell, and the greatest gift of all – the power of thought.

'Go into Middle Earth,' said the gods. 'Fill it with your children, and make it into a world of people.'

Then Odin, Vili and Ve created Asgard, the heavenly home of the gods. They built a rainbow bridge called Bifrost to link Asgard with Middle Earth so that they could visit the world of people whenever they pleased.

Ragnarok, the End of the Gods

The gods gathered in the hall of Valhalla. As they took their seats, they glanced curiously at the Seeress who crouched by the hearth. Odin, chief of the gods, had summoned her from her endless sleep, deep under the earth.

'Seeress,' said Odin, 'tell us what is to be. What will be the fate of the gods?'

The Seeress lifted her head and the leaping flames of the fire cast strange shadows upon her face as she spoke:

'In the days to come, the world will grow old and the gods will grow old with it. Their strength will begin to fail. Evil spirits that hide now in the shadows and the forests and the dark places of the world will grow strong. They will walk openly in sunlight, spreading chaos among humankind. Kings will be slain by their subjects and, in the wars that follow, good will be overturned. Brother will turn against brother, parents will betray their children, and the rivers will run red with spilt blood.

'The great ghost-wolf, Fenrir, will leap into the sky and devour the Sun and Moon with his iron jaws. There will be darkness, and the world will be held in the grip of a bitter winter that will last for three long years. The stars will fall from

the sky in fiery showers. Glaciers will grind the mountains into dust. The earth will heave, and shake, and split. All the monsters that lie imprisoned in the Underworld will escape, and the gates of the Hall of Hell will open wide, dripping with venom, hungry for the feast of souls that will come.

'The serpent Midgarsormr will rise from the depths of the ocean. Its lashing tail will raise tidal waves to flood the land. Across the black, stormy waters will sail Naglfar, the Ship of Death, built of dead men's nails. Loki, God of Mischief, will steer it and with him he will carry the Frost Giants, all eager for battle.

'The fire demon, Surt, will march his armies out of Muspellheim, Land of Fire. They will fall upon the rainbow bridge that joins the two worlds of the gods and the humans, and destroy it. Then all the hosts of demons, monsters and giants will gather on the plains of Valhalla, and the sound of their howling will shake the foundations of Asgard.

'The god Heimdal will blow his horn, and Odin will lead the army of the gods out to their doom – for this will be the day of Ragnarok, the end of the gods. In that battle, each god must face his deadliest enemy. Odin will fight with Fenrir. Thor will be wrapped in Midgarsormr's crushing coils. Freyr will meet with Surt, and Heimdal will combat the treacherous Loki. Each will slay the other until only Surt remains. With his dying breath, Surt will fill the world with fire. The bodies of the dead will burn to ash and the last humans will perish, until at last the world vanishes beneath the eternal waters of the sea...'

There was silence in the hall. The gods sat grim-faced, shuddering as they thought about their terrible fate. Some gazed into the hearth, seeing in its flames a presage of the dreadful fire to come.

At last, Odin said, 'Is this all, Seeress? Will the world we have made come to death and nothing? Is there no hope?'

A log shifted in the hearth, and as a shower of sparks danced up into the gathering shadows, the Seeress spoke again:

'This world is nothing but a tiny twig of Ygdrassil, the Universe Tree. In time, a new twig will grow in its place and a new Earth will rise from the waters, fresh and green. Balder the Beautiful will return from the dead to form a new race of gods and Ygdrassil will bear two fruits – a man and a woman. Their names will be Lif and Lifdrassr, and their descendants will fill the world with people.'

'But wait!' cried Odin. 'This new world, these new gods and people – will they be better than the ones that went before?'

The Seeress smiled sadly.

'That is not for you to know,' she said.

Who's who?

ADAM Hebrew. The first man. Created by Jehovah, husband of Eve. Pages 10–11.

AJE Nigerian. Daughter of Olodumare. Transformed into a hen to help with the creation of the world. Pages 52, 54.

AMEI AWI Borneoan. God of farming. Husband of Burung Une. His children climb a mountain to decide the fate of humankind. Pages 49–51.

AMMA Dogon. Creator of the world and the first humans. Amma forges the Sun and Moon in his smithy. Pages 78, 79, 80.

ANGELS (THE SEVEN) Christian. The seven angels blow trumpets to herald the different stages of the destruction of the world. Pages 14–15.

ANSHAR Babylonian. God of the place where the Earth touches the sky. Offspring of Lahnu and Lahanu. Page 24.

ANU Babylonian. The sky god. Offspring of Anshar and Kishar. Pages 25, 27.

APSU Babylonian. God of the primeval fresh-water sea. Husband of Tiamat, father of Mummu and Kingu. Pages 24, 25.

ASKR Norse. The first man. Created from a tree by Odin, Vili and Ve. Page 88.

ATLAS Greek. A Titan who was punished by the gods. He was sentenced to hold the weight of the sky on his shoulders for all eternity. Page 41.

ATUM Egyptian. Creator of light and the first land and people. Creator of Shu and Tefnut. Pages 16–19.

AUDUMLA Norse. The primeval cow. Her licking of the frozen giant Ymir brings forth the Frost Giants and the Norse gods Odin, Vili and Ve. Page 87.

BAGADJIMBIRI BROTHERS Australian Aborigine. Dingo Ancestors and also Ancestors of rain clouds and water snakes. Makers of the first water-holes. Pages 70–3.

BALDER THE BEAUTIFUL Norse. The god who will return from the dead to remake the world after the destruction of the gods. Page 92.

BURUNG UNE Borneoan. Goddess of farming. Wife of Amei Awi. Her children climb a mountain to decide the destiny of humankind. Pages 49–51.

COYOTE Native North American. Creator of the world. In many legends, Coyote appears as a cunning trickster. Pages 44–7.

CRONOS Greek. Most powerful of the Titans and father of the gods, all of whom he swallows at birth, save Zeus. Son of Gea and Uranos, whom he kills, Cronos is killed in turn by his own son, Zeus. Pages 37–41.

CYCLOPSES Greek. One-eyed giants, children of Gea and Uranos, makers of the Underworld. Pages 37, 38, 41.

DAMINKA Babylonian. Created by the god Ea as his wife. Mother of Marduk. Page 25.

DEMETER Greek. Goddess of agriculture, sister of Zeus, daughter of Cronos and Rhea. Page 40.

EA Babylonian. God of Earth and water. Father of Marduk. Pages 25, 29.

EMBLA Norse. The first woman. Created from a tree by the gods Odin, Vili and Ve. Wife of Askr. Page 88.

ENLIL Babylonian. The god who intends to destroy humankind in a great flood. His plan is thwarted by the god Ea. Pages 28–31.

EVE Hebrew. The first woman, created by Jehovah. Wife of Adam. Pages 10–11.

FENRIR Norse. The spirit wolf who will swallow the Sun and Moon at the end of the world. The mortal enemy of Odin. Pages 89, 91.

FREYR Norse. In the last battle of the gods, Freyr will be slain by his great enemy Surt, the fire demon. Page 91.

FROST GIANTS Norse. They spring from the body of Ymir. They are war-like beings who constantly seek to destroy the world made by the Norse gods. Pages 87–8, 91.

GEA Greek. First goddess of the Earth, which she brings out of chaos. Wife of Uranos and mother of the Giants, Cyclopses and Titans. Pages 36, 37, 38.

GIANTS (HUNDRED-HANDED) Greek. Offspring of Gea and Uranos. Shapers of the land. Pages 37, 38. 41.

GREAT ONE Zulu. Creator of the world, the Bantu people and white races. Great One intends that humans should live forever, but his intention is thwarted by Lizard. Pages 57–8.

GUCAMATZ Mayan. One of the Feathered Gods who plans and builds the world with Tepeu. Pages 66–9.

HADES Greek. God of the Underworld. Son of Cronos and Rhea, brother of Zeus. Page 40.

HEIMDAL Norse. The god whose war horn will summon the gods to their last battle. Mortal enemy of Loki. Page 91.

HERA Greek. Sister/wife of the god Zeus, daughter of Cronos and Rhea. Page 40.

HESTIA Greek. Goddess of the hearth, sister of Zeus, daughter of Cronos and Rhea. Page 40.

HIGH LORD OF HEAVEN Japanese. One of the chief gods, creator of Izanagi and Izanami, the first man and woman. Page 32.

HURAKAN Mayan. God of winds, storms, breath and floods. Carries out the creation plan of Gucamatz and Tepeu and gives life to the first humans. Pages 66–9.

IZANAGI Japanese. The first man. Created by the High Lord of Heaven. Husband of Izanami. Stirs the primeval ocean with a magic spear and creates the islands of Japan. Pages 32–3.

IZANAMI Japanese. The first woman. Created by the High Lord of Heaven. Wife of Izanagi, whom she helps to create Japan. Pages 32–3.

JEHOVAH Hebrew. The Supreme God, creator of the Universe and humankind. Jehovah intends humans to live in happiness forever, but this plan is spoiled by the disobedience of Adam and Eve. Pages 8–15.

KINGU Babylonian. Son of Apsu and Tiamat. Slain by Marduk, his blood is used for the creation of animals and people. Pages 24, 25 27.

KISHAR Babylonian. God of the place where the sky touches the Earth, offspring of Lahnu and Lahanu. Pages 24, 25.

LAHANU Babylonian. One of twin gods born to Apsu and Tiamat, parent of Anshar and Kishar. Page 24.

LAHNU Babylonian. One of twin gods born to Apsu and Tiamat, parent of Anshar and Kishar. Page 24.

LAMB OF GOD Christian. The lamb with seven horns and seven eyes who breaks the seven seals on the book given to him by Jehovah and begins the destruction of the world. Page 12.

LOKI Norse. God of mischief. He will betray the gods to the Frost Giants. Mortal enemy of Heimdal. Page 91.

LUONNATAR Finnish. Mother of the world. She assists in its creation and shapes the land. Pages 34–5.

MARDUK Babylonian. A warrior-god. Son of Ea and Daminka. Defeats the army of the goddess Tiamat and uses her body to make the Earth. Creates animals and people from the blood of Kingu, Tiamat's son. Pages 25–7.

MAWU Dahomey. Creator of Rainbow Snake and the world. Pages 74–7.

MIDGARSORMR Norse. The great sea-serpent who will rise from the oceans and flood the land before the last battle of the gods. Mortal enemy of Thor. Page 91.

MUMMU Babylonian. Son of Apsu and Tiamat. Pages 24, 25.

NGARIMAN Australian Aborigine. Ancestor of the cat, slayer of the Bagadjimbiri brothers. Pages 72–3.

NUMMO (THE) Dogon. Children of the creator god, Amma, and Earth. The Nummo are twins, one male, one female. Their upper halves are human and their lower halves are snake-like. The Nummo create the ancestors of all the peoples of the world. Pages 79–81.

NUT Egyptian. The sacred cow who carries the gods into the sky at the time of their deaths. Page 23.

OBTALA Nigerian. Son of Olodumare. Helps to create the world. First being to become drunk after making palm wine, creator of the Sun and Moon. Pages 52, 54, 55.

ODIN Norse. Chief of the Norse gods, creator of the world and humans and brother of Vili and Ve. Licked from the frozen Ymir by the cow Audumla. Pages 87–8, 89–92.

ODUDUWA Nigerian. Daughter of Olodumare. Transformed into a pigeon to assist with the creation of the world. Pages 52, 54.

OLODUMARE Nigerian. Creator of the world and the Yoruba people. Father of Aje, Obtala and Oduduwa. Pages 52–5.

ONE (THE) Hindu. The creator of the Universe. The One splits itself into the first man and woman, so filling the world with life. Pages 64–5.

PAN KU Chinese. A giant being. As he dies, his body is tranformed into the physical world and the elements. Pages 59–61.

POSEIDON Greek. God of the Sea. Son of Cronos and Rhea and brother of Zeus. Page 40.

RA Egyptian. Greatest of the Egyptian gods, his birth is foretold by Atum. Pages 19, 20–3.

RAINBOW SNAKE Dahomey. First creation of Mawu. Rainbow Snake helps in the creation of the world and holds the land up out of the sea. Pages 75–7.

RHEA Greek. A Titan. Daughter of Uranos and Gea, wife of Cronos and mother of the gods. She rescues her son Zeus and keeps him hidden until he is strong enough to oppose his father, Cronos. Pages 38, 40.

RIDERS (THE FOUR) Christian. they are Conquest, Famine, War and Death. They are loosed by the Lamb of God to begin the destruction of the world. Pages 12–13.

SEERESS (THE) Norse. The Seeress recounts to the gods the story of their ultimate destruction. Pages 89–92.

SEKHMET Egyptian. The lion-goddess sent by Ra to destroy all humans. When Ra relents, Sekhmet is tricked into drinking a lake of beer. She falls asleep and humans are saved. Pages 21–3.

SERAU Dogon. The first man, created by the Nummo. Serau steals from the forge of the god Amma, but in the attempt he scatters all the peoples of the world far and wide. Pages 80, 81.

SERPENT (THE) Hebrew. The Serpent tempts Adam and Eve to eat the fruit of the Tree of Knowledge and disobey Jehovah. Pages 10–11.

SHU Egyptian. God of wind and breath, created by Atum. Pages 17, 18, 19.

SURT Norse. Lord of the fire demons of Muspellheim. Mortal enemy of the god, Freyr. Page 91.

TAAROA Tahitian. Creator of the world, which comes from his own being. Page 62.

TEFNUT Egyptian. Goddess of water. Created by Atum. Pages 17, 18, 19.

TEPEU Mayan. One of the Feathered Gods. Plans the world with Gucamatz and creates it with the aid of Hurakan. Pages 66–9.

THOR Norse. God of thunder. In the last battle of the gods, Thor is slain as he kills the sea-serpent Midgarsormr. Page 91.

TIAMAT Babylonian. Goddess of the ocean, wife of Apsu. She battles for control of creation with Marduk. When she is defeated and slain, Marduk makes the world from her body. Pages 24–7.

TITANS Greek. Six males and six females, children of Gea and Uranos. They battle with the gods for control of creation. Pages 37, 38, 40, 41.

URANOS Greek. God of the sky. He mates with Gea and fathers the hundred-handed giants, the Cyclopses and the Titans. Overthrown and slain by his son, Cronos. Pages 36, 37, 38.

UTNAPISHTIM Babylonian. Warned of the anger of the god Enlil by Ea, Utnapishtim builds a boat and fills it with animals and his family, so ensuring the survival of humankind. Pages 29, 31.

VE Norse. Brother of Odin and Vili, born from the body of Ymir by the licking of Audumla, the primeval cow. Ve assists his brothers in creating the world and the first people. Pages 87–8.

VILI Norse. Brother of Odin and Ve, born from the body of Ymir by the licking of Audumla, the primeval cow. Vili assists his brothers in creating the world and the first people. Pages 87–8.

WALKING MAN Native North American. Walking Man creates the world, the Sun and Moon from dust and water. Pages 42–3.

YMIR Norse. A frozen giant floating in the ocean of Ginnungagap, his body is licked by the cow Audumla and brings forth the Frost Giants and the gods, Odin, Vili and Ve. The gods use Ymir's body to make the world. Pages 87–8.

ZEUS Greek. Chief of the gods, and god of the thunderbolt. Son of Rhea and Cronos, whom he defeats in battle and slays. Brother of Demeter, Hera, Hestia, Hades and Poseidon. Pages 38–41.